Copyrighted Material

Published by: Tyler Hollis Publishing
www.childrensbookillustrator-tylerhollis.com

Author: Joanne Dott Stearns

Illustrator: Tyler Hollis

From: Me!
Joanne
Enjoy!
Love.
12/25/17

MW00898731

DEDICATION

To Becca who inspired this book,
to Mom, who taught me to love reading
and teaching, to Susan, who made it
possible to travel to other-worldly
Antarctica, and to my loving husband,
Marshall, who helps me live the
impossible dream. Deep gratitude to
Janet for her technical skills and
friendship, and to Debbie, Mona,
Gloria, Joan, Bette, Barbara, Lorrie,
and Iris for making my life happier
and sillier.
A big thank you to Tyler Hollis for
her beautiful illustrations and
publishing expertise.

Author ~ Joanne Dott Stearns

Joanne Dott Stearns was an elementary school teacher for 15 years with experience teaching all grade levels and adults, and an elementary school principal for 18 years. She has been retired since 2003. Joanne is a world-wide traveler and considers Antarctica

to be the most wondrous and incredible place on Earth. She hopes her next trip is to Africa. Her husband Marshall is also a retired school principal, and they live in Port St. Lucie, Florida, in a retirement community. Joanne grew up in Pennsylvania with her parents and two brothers who continue to live in Pennsylvania. She is the lucky grandmother of Rebecca, who is now 10 years old. Becca, her granddaughter, is the main character in *The Penguin's Secret*.

THE PENGUIN'S SECRET

To begin this story:

I'm Gamma Jo. My granddaughter, Becca and I were on a huge cruise ship travelling the sea on our way to a far off land called Antarctica. Antarctica is on the other side of the world. That's how **far** away it is.

CREATURES THAT LIVE ON EACH SIDE OF THE POLES

* Polar Bear-Orca Whale-Variety of Whales-Seals
Walrus-Wolf-Fox-Caribou-Reindeer-Musk Ox-

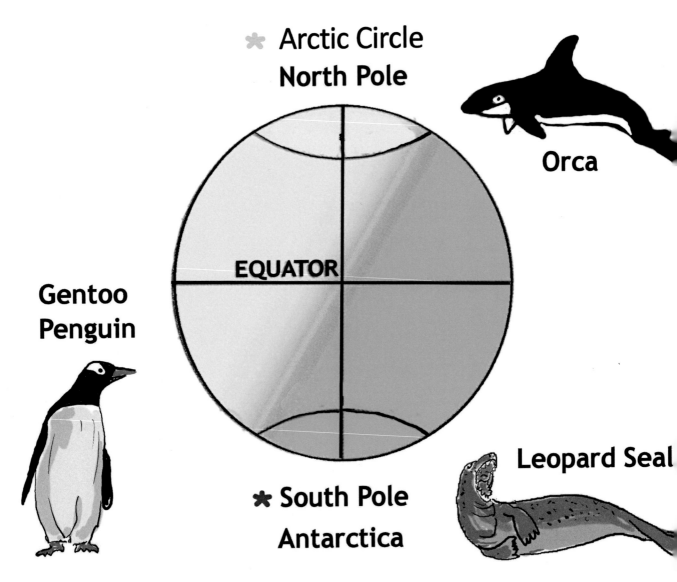

* Arctic Circle
North Pole

Orca

Gentoo
Penguin

EQUATOR

Leopard Seal

* South Pole
Antarctica

*Orca Whale-Variety of Whales-Elephant Seal-
Variety of Seals-Penguins/Adelie-Chinstrap-
Emperor-Gentoo-King-Macaroni
The Antarctica is the coldest place on earth.
Orca Whales and Leopard Seals eat Penguins.

Antarctica is a land of snow, ice, icebergs, mountains of ice, seals, whales, and of course, penguins! There are no trees, grass, or dirt on Antarctica. It looks like a winter wonderland all year long. Sometimes the icy cliffs and icebergs look blue, but mainly, it's a white colored world. Antarctica's ice can be one mile thick. Only about 1000 to 5000 people live there because it's way too cold.

The ship we travelled on was a large ocean liner that circled around the world. We had a cabin on the ship. The couch in the living room turned into a bed at night. That's where Becca and I slept each night. During the day, the bed became a couch again. It was very comfortable.

The best part of the cabin was the balcony. The balcony of an ocean liner is like a floating porch that is attached to the living room and is outside. Large sliding glass doors separate the living room and the balcony, and the indoors and the outdoors.

Each day, Becca and I would sit outside on the balcony in deck chairs and watch the ocean world go by. It was usually very cold! Most days were below freezing temperatures. In Antarctica, it feels like winter all the time.

It was fun to watch the ship plow through the water. From the balcony, we got to see many wild and amazing sea creatures like whales, seals, and of course, penguins! Seeing Antarctica from the balcony was magical and wondrous.

Penguins are family creatures. They love being all together. In fact, that's part of the secret! The awful part!

Now, don't flip ahead to the next pages to see what the big secret of the penguins is, because I have to give you a few facts about penguins first. You will be amazed! Truly!

Penguins want to be with their family most of the time. They cuddle and stay together for life. The only time a penguin leaves her family is to hunt for food. Penguins eat small fish and squid. Mommas feed their babies by vomiting the catch into their mouths. They do this to soften the food for the babies so eating is easy, and the food just glides down their throats.

Baby penguins are covered in

Fur,

and often *snuggle* their parents.

To get their food from the ocean, penguins dive off the icy cliffs, and it looks like they are flying. But penguins don't fly. It's an awesome sight to see the penguins swim so fast, and come up out of the water in an arc, and quickly dive back into the sea.

Now, the penguin has a ginormous, huge, gigantic, BIG secret!

But no one EVER talks about it!
You will never, never guess what it is in a billion, trillion, gazillion years.

And I mean it!

And it's GROSS, too! Really!

Ready for the secret?

Here it is!

POOP! PENGUIN POOP!

It was soooooooooooooooooo stinky!

The poop smell was EVERYWHERE!

Who knew?

And we haven't seen
a single penguin yet!

YUCKY!

We started to hold our noses, and tried to catch a breath of fresh air, but it was useless. As our ship was nearing the **thousands and thousands** of penguins on land, the odor got stronger!

It was unbelievable! The living, breathing mass of penguin bodies was everywhere... like little black dots on the white land.

And poop was everywhere.

And our ship was getting closer and closer to land.

If the poop smelled this bad on the ship, Becca and I couldn't imagine how badly it would smell on land! And the captain was announcing that we were stopping to drop anchor.

We were **actually** going to get into small rubber boats with motors called zodiacs, and sail to the mainland and see the penguins up close.

Because Antarctica is very, very, very cold, when anyone would want to get off the ship, he or she would have to wear **extremely** heavy winter coats, and boots, sweaters, underwear, gloves, and hats.

We would all go through an inspection when it was time to get into the zodiacs, because we had to show our ship's captain we were dressed properly. If we were not dressed properly for the cold weather, we weren't allowed to leave the ship.

We could FREEZE and get ill.

Sometimes, Becca and I had on so many layers of clothing, we could **barely** move our arms and legs!

It was cold riding the zodiac, but seeing the penguins was **outstanding**.
They looked so sweet and never minded we were there.

They just **trotted** and waddled past us

in lines of two,

three,

or as many as 15 in a row.

Really, penguin poop was everywhere!

Penguin poop can be at least three different colors...pink, green, and **black,** and depends upon what the penguin eats.

Unlike other animals that leave their poop in mounds, penguin colored poop is *watery* and *leaks* into the snow and ice and

drips down the mountains of ICE .

When penguins poop, it can

spray

up to two feet away!

And sometimes

it hits other penguins nearby!

On all our travels around Antarctica, we could always tell when the ship was nearing penguin land, because we could always smell the penguin poop from FAAAAAAR AWAY....way before we could SEE them! The more penguins, the bigger the stink!

After being with thousands and hundreds of thousands of penguins,

we enjoyed seeing them WAY more than smelling them!

And, so now you know the secret of the penguins. Truly, very, very few people know the secret of the penguin.

And, now, you do, too!

Lucky, lucky, you!

But, don't tell! It's a secret!

FUN FACTS OFANTARCTICA

*Antarctica means "other arctic" because
  Antarctica is home to the South Pole, and
  it looks like a frozen ocean;
* Has its own Southern Lights (Aurora Australis)
  while the Northern Lights are called the
  Aurora Borealis ;
*Has icebergs which are huge hunks of ice that have
  broken off from the icy shelf;
*Has icebergs that float as small pieces of ice and can
  be as big as 25 to 100 miles in area; icebergs can look
  crystal clear, white, blue, green, pink, and brown;
  they can have caves, icicles, grottos, or arches;
* Is the coldest, driest, windiest continent on Earth,
  and has the highest elevation of all the continents;
*Is a desert because it only gets about 8 inches of
  rain a year;
*Has temperatures that can be as low as minus 129
  degrees F in the winter months of June, July and August
  and up to 41-59 degrees on its beaches during the
  summer months of January, February, and March;
*Is 98% ice that can be one mile thick and its ice
  encircles the South Pole (radio soundings recorded ice
  at 2 miles/704 inches thick from the Wilkes Land coast

*Has no permanent humans living there because of the harsh weather; however 1000-5000 people reside there for scientific study to conduct experiments, and to assist in keeping mail services and other research stations open;

*Has food and supplies flown in by airplane once a month during the summer, and once every three months in the winter;

*Has a peace treaty signed by 49 countries that promises to have no wartime activities, no nuclear wastes, and no activities that could destroy the ecosystem, and no country owns it;

*Takes 18 hours from Los Angeles, CA to fly to Santiago, Chile, and then onto Ushuaia, Argentina to embark onto a large ship that can sail to Antarctica;

*Has a small amount of insects and plants, but no trees;

*Has seals, penguins, whales, dolphins, porpoises, gulls and terns, albatrosses, petrels, cormorants, and other birds, but NO polar bears (Polar bears are only in the North Pole.);

*Has only four different species of penguins that breed there---the Emperor, the Adelie, the Chinstrap, and the Gentoo.

FUN FACTS ABOUT ANTARTCICA'S PENGUINS

*There are about 16-20 different kinds of penguins.

*The Emperor penguins are the largest of all penguins, and you can see many of them in the film "March of the Penguins".

*Penguins eat krill, sardines, squid, and anchovies.

*Penguins drink sea water.

*Killer whales (Orca), some seals (mostly Leopard seals), and sharks eat penguins.

*Oil spills kill penguins.

*Penguins are an endangered species.

*Penguins can be seen in the wild in South Africa, Australia, New Zealand, Chile, Argentina, the Galapagos Islands, and Antarctica.

*Penguins cannot breathe underwater, but they can store oxygen in their bodies that allows them to swim underwater for long periods, and they walk upright like we do.

*Penguins can leap out of the water like porpoises.

*Penguins cannot fly even though they have feathers and wings and are considered birds.

The World
Certificate of Landing
Antarctic Expedition
2007

This certificate serves to witness that

Joanne Stearns

set foot upon the shores of Antarctica while sailing on *MV The World*
in January 2007 to a southern lattitude of 67° 9' 1 s

Master of *The World*
Captain Dap Saevik

Expedition Leader
Geoff Green

General Manager of *The World*
Mc Michael Brooks

CERTIFICADO

Se otorga el siguiente certificado al Sr. (a) Joanne Stearns
por haber, efectuado el cruce al Cabo de Hornos Lat. 55°58's, G. 067°15'w.

Cabo de hornos a 30 *dias del mes de* enero *del 2007*

ISLA HORNOS
3 0 ENE. 2007
CHILE
CABO DE HORNOS

Alcalde de Mar
Isla cabo de Hornos

REGIÓN DE MAGALLANES Y ANTÁRTICA CHILENA

CAPE HORN

REFERENCES

Mackay, James. (Ed.) World Facts (2003). Barnes and Noble Books.

McGonigal, David., Woodworth, Lynn. Antarctica: The Blue Continent. (2003). Buffalo, NY: Firefly Books Inc.

Momatiuk, Yva., Eastcott, John. Face to Face with Penguins. (2009) Washington, D.C.: National Geographic Society.

Illustrator ~ Tyler Hollis

Tyler Hollis is a well-known children's illustrator and publisher. Her style is considered to be the "old fashion" Golden Book that stays sweet and simple and connects with both children and adults. She does her line work in pen and her coloring on the computer with a pallet of colors she developed herself. She is inspired by childhood memories. Tyler has been interviewed on ABC, NBC, and CBS for her illustration talents. She is a member of SCBWI.

Tyler Hollis website:
www.childrensbookillustrator-tylerhollis.com
faeryring@bellsouth.com

Made in the USA
Middletown, DE
19 January 2015